BADGE BUTTON PIN

By Gavin Lucas

LAURENCE KING

Published in 2007 by
Laurence King Publishing Ltd
4th Floor, 361–373 City Road
London EC1V 1LR
United Kingdom
enquiries@laurenceking.co.uk
www.laurenceking.co.uk

Copyright © text 2007
Gavin Lucas

All rights reserved. No part
of this publication may be
reproduced or transmitted in
any form or by any means,
electronic or mechanical,
including photocopy,
recording or any information
storage and retrieval system,
without prior permission in
writing from the publisher.

A catalogue record for this
book is available from the
British Library.

ISBN-13: 978-1-85669-409-4
ISBN-10: 1-85669-409-7

Special edition
ISBN-13: 978-1-85669-517-6
ISBN-10: 1-85669-517-4

Designed by Intercity
www.intercitydesign.com

Printed in China

11 DECORATIVE
37 PROMOTIONAL
63 PACKS
87 WEBSITES
109 ART

A range of badge-making machines can be found and ordered easily online – most are inexpensive. Here are some websites that offer a variety of such devices:

www.buybuttonparts.com
www.badgemachine.co.uk
www.craftdepot.co.uk
www.buttonsonline.com
www.badgeaminit.com
www.badgeworx.com
www.londonemblem.com

IN THE FOLLOWING PAGES YOU WILL FIND A SELECTION OF BADGES MADE IN THE LAST FEW YEARS BY SOME OF THE MOST POPULAR AND RESPECTED ARTISTS, DESIGNERS AND ILLUSTRATORS WORKING TODAY. SOME WERE MADE FOR THE FUN OF IT, SOME FOR PROMOTIONAL OR MARKETING PURPOSES. ALL ARE SMALL, SHINY, ROUND PIECES OF WEARABLE ART. WHICH IS YOUR FAVOURITE – AND WHO DESIGNED IT? FASHION DESIGNERS ANTONI & ALISON? ARTIST IAN WRIGHT? GRAPHIC DESIGNER MILTON GLASER, PERHAPS? THERE IS A BADGE FOR EVERY OCCASION AND EVERYONE, APART PERHAPS FOR THOSE SUFFERING WITH ENETOPHOBIA. AND IF YOU BELIEVE THERE ISN'T A BADGE FOR YOU, WHAT'S STOPPING YOU FROM DESIGNING ONE YOURSELF?

Whether you love The White Stripes, are a member of Greenpeace, had something to do with Blue Peter or simply support a maxim such as "Down With Pants" (and who could blame you?), pinning a badge – or button or pin, if you're reading in the US – has long been a means of communicating personal taste or opinion.

"For something so small, the badge holds great power," claims Darren Firth, founder of badge-dedicated website Wearitwithpride.com. Spotting that there was no central destination where badges could be bought, either on the street or online, and regretting the "clear lack of design-time that goes into badges", Firth set up his site in 2003. It now features over 170 badges designed by the likes of Jon Burgerman, Büro Destruct, David Horvath, Insect and Pixel Surgeon.

Wear It With Pride has received well over 100,000 hits over the last year, demonstrating the current pulling power of the badge. But although badges have become noticeably fashionable again over the last two or three years, Firth insists: "There is a niche group of people who will always buy badges."

In the UK alone, there are now several sites that champion the button badge, set up not by historical badge collectors but rather by young creatives keen to show off their take on badge design. Check out Pinpops.com, set up and run by badge and sticker enthusiast Dom Murphy of TAK!, or Stereohype.com's By Invitation Only badge activity, courtesy of design duo FL@33, or Prickie.com.

A host of designers, including Airside, Michael C. Place's Build and Alexander Gelman's Design Machine, now produce their own badges, in the same way they might have ideas for and create T-shirts.

The button badge phenomenon began with the invention of celluloid. The first cheap badges were produced in 1896 by American promotional products manufacturer Whitehead & Hoag, a New Jersey company that had just come up with a new process for making buttons for clothing. This involved placing cloth on top of a round, flanged piece of metal and stamping it so that a circular metal collar was lodged into the back of the "button", gripping the cloth tightly in the process. In fact, this is the reason why the one-inch button badge is called a "button" in the US to this day. In the first year of celluloid badge production, over a million were made – celebrating football stars, actors and actresses – and given away with packs of cigarettes.

In the 1950s, badges promoting holiday camps, comics, social clubs and products became popular in the UK. The 60s saw the badge become a vehicle for anti-establishment slogans, while the 70s saw it all really take off with the explosion of punk, a movement that was as much about fashion as it was about music.

London-based artist and collector of "essential ephemera" Mark Pawson has been making badges for the best part of 20 years. "In the late 70s and early 80s, Better Badges, a badge shop on the Caledonian Road, always had an ad on the back page of the weekly music paper the *NME*," he recalls. "Each week the ad contained an updated badge chart."

Further reading:

The Official Badge Collector's Guide: From the 1890s to the 1980s by Frank R. Setchfield. Published by Longman, 1986

Badges by Philip Attwood. Published by the British Museum Press, 2004

Pawson's website, at www.mpawson.demon.co.uk, demonstrates his enduring interest in badges. His handmade sets come in packs of four "to make them more presentable". Some are based around a slogan, some are made up of found symbols or icons, while others feature patterns found on the insides of envelopes or on Japanese origami paper. These represent, he says, "a move towards making badges more like jewellery, more decorative". So what does Pawson make of current badge interest? "Mine are still selling good and steady," he reveals, "but it does seem that more people have got hold of their own badge-making machines. One trendy magazine recently had a 'win your own badge machine' competition in conjunction with a badge machine manufacturer."

As well as being used as decorative fashion accessories and to make political or social statements, the badge has the potential to play a vital role in both campaigning and income generation, something the music industry has long been aware of. Badges are cheap and easy to make and can be sold cheaply to provide some all-important capital for a touring band on a knife-edge budget. The charity sector also uses badges to generate revenue. The success of entire campaigns can rest on the badge's combination of message-spreading and fund-generating qualities. "The number of charities that use this form of marketing is huge – as are the quantities of badges (up to 100,000 per batch) being manufactured for them," says Daniel Lyons, managing director of London-based manufacturer Rocket Badge, which has a dedicated charities division.

But there are other potential uses for the badge that are still to be explored. "Linking badges with inexpensive information-storing and transmitting technologies makes the future of badges as marketing tools bright," says Lyons.

For instance, in 2005 designer Jeremy Mac Lynn and Daniel Charny developed the art direction for Sharewear, a badge for people who want to be heard clearly by people using hearing aids. When the technology is ready, the badges will enable short-distance transmission of the wearer's voice directly to the aid, overriding surrounding noises.

Ian Wright has been working with the badge as an art medium for a number of years. In May 2006 his *Mass Production* exhibition opened at New York's Christopher Henry Gallery. It featured five portraits of pop-culture icons, each measuring 49 by 64½ inches, rendered using over 2,500 one-inch button badges. Playing with the idea of digital imagery, the buttons become pixels – albeit ones which have been painstakingly hand-crafted. Each work was priced at a very cool $15,000.

The key to the badge's enduring popularity lies in its adaptability to suit different projects. Really the only thing limiting what you can do with badges is your imagination – which is why button badges have been around for so long and will continue to be popular for many years to come.

We asked nine contributors to Badge/Button/Pin to produce a one-inch button badge design unique to this project.

FL@33
This design by FL@33 is called Marble. "Badges are very much like the glass marbles we used to play with as children," says FL@33's Tomi Vollauschek. "They are usually part of a collection where some are added, others are lost or exchanged while each is an individual object of beauty."

Kim Jones
"This badge is based on my love of dogs and my obsession with Pop Art and music," reveals fashion designer Kim Jones. "Was Dog a Doughnut? by Cat Stevens is the inspiration."

Fred Deakin
"A badge machine gives you such power," enthuses designer, musician and badge-lover Fred Deakin of design studio Airside. "You can make your fantasy band real; all it takes is one badge with their logo on your lapel and you're competing with The Strokes. Instant disposable art that makes you new friends. You gotta love badges!"

Michael C. Place/Build
Designer Michael C. Place of studio Build created this split-personality badge specially for this book.

Trevor Jackson
Designer, DJ, musician and self-confessed "know-it-all and good-for-nothing," Trevor Jackson designed this badge for us and sent the accompanying message: "One inch, not much to say, not much space to fit it in. Don't wanna think too much, let's be honest, time for a change."

Antoni & Alison
Antoni & Alison designed this Elvis badge several years ago but have reversed the colour for this re-release of the design. "The blue was – and always is – based on Yves Klein blue (International Klein Blue)," they tell us, "so that we reference two of our most revered people in one badge."

Alexander Gelman
Alexander Gelman, or just plain Gelman to his friends, loves buttons. So much so, he designed this "button" for us. Get it?

Femke Hiemstra
"This strange long-eared poodle is one of my recent sketches which I thought would fit well on a badge," explains Dutch artist Femke Hiemstra. "A badge is a great, hip accessory. I like them a lot and use them to personalize my clothes and, quite often, to pimp up my bag!"

Mark Pawson
This badge by London-based artist Mark Pawson is called My Favourite Shirt. He actually designed three different versions for us.

DECORATIVE

JAN KALLWEJT

Designer Jan Kallwejt hails from Warsaw and works in print and also interactive design. His first set of badges was entitled Fusters; each features a graphically represented creature in white on a red ground. Soon to follow was his Embryo set and still more… Bright, colourful and fun, Kallwejt's badges can be viewed on his website.

www.kallwejt.com

NAJA CONRAD-HANSEN

Naja Conrad-Hansen graduated in 2003 from the Danish Design School where she focused on illustration, graphic design, building fashion concepts and silkscreen printing. Now a freelance designer based in Copenhagen, her studio is called Meannorth and it is under this name that her badge designs can be found and purchased from website Prickie.com (see page 94).

"I see badges as part of the fashion world," she tells us, "where you can freely express opinions or display images. The combination of a safety pin and an image is one of the most brilliant ideas ever."

www.meannorth.com

MARCUS OAKLEY

"I like the idea of a badge, how you can write little messages or positive slogans or just have a happy illustration," says UK-based illustrator Marcus Oakley, who sometimes goes by the name Mr Werewolf and is represented by artist agency the CWC Group.

These particular badges all celebrate the wildlife of the English undergrowth. "I often like to think of woodlands as being magical places and that the creatures who live there can talk and enjoy drinking tea," says Oakley.

www.banjo.dircon.co.uk/mrwerewolf.mrw1.html
www.cwctokyo.com (Asia)
www.cwc-i.com (United States and Europe)

WHAT WHAT

Twins John and Edward Harrison work under the name What What. When not designing badges, they work together producing weird and wonderful illustrations and designs.

"We started doing badges as a promotional tool about three years ago," explains John. "We thought it'd be much better to give away badges as opposed to flat and boring business cards. We bought a badge machine and we were soon coming up with loads of designs." After handing out a thousand badges for free, the pair decided to start selling them, initially on their website. Now What What badges can be found throughout England in shops such as Magma, Playlounge and the ICA store.

"Whenever we go travelling and meet new people we give them a badge so that they remember us," adds John. "We continually come up with new designs for our shop and occasionally make one-off badges for friends. We love the challenge of creating images that work on such a small scale, but most of all we love seeing people wear our badges."

www.whatwhat.co.uk

RE-PSYCHE

Athens-based Dimitris Emmanouil works as a
designer under the moniker Paranormale –
unless he's doing badges, in which case he
goes by the name Re-psyche. His badges are
made using a range of techniques and almost
all of them are one-offs created using vintage
fabrics or vintage lithographic prints. A few are
also made by photocopying textures, materials
and printed matter.

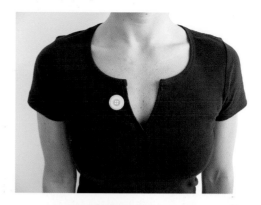

RIEME.NL

Rieme Gleijm studied graphic design in both the Netherlands and at London's Royal College of Art. She currently lives and works in the Netherlands where she produces mainly print-based work under the name Rieme.nl. She created this series of colourful button badges entitled Button Up for Stereohype's third By Invitation Only badge project (see page 98).

www.rieme.nl

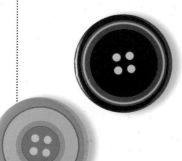

ANTONI & ALISON

"We have always, from as early as we can remember, loved and collected badges," reveals Antoni Burakowski, one half of fashion label Antoni & Alison. Together with A&A's other half, Alison Roberts, he drew up the following list of reasons why:

● You can wear them on your normal clothes – and a badge will give you style and attitude.
● The fact that they are put-on-able and take-off-able statements (so you can easily change your mind).
● They are cheap (sometimes free) and so available to everyone.
● You can be a fan/show allegiance to anything and everything and have it put on a badge and wear it in a minimalist one-inch or maximalist five-inch way. (A&A have a whopping five-inch badge depicting Elvis in their collection.)
● They are usually round – and most things look and work well in a circle.
● They are like little pieces of Pop Art.
● Protest badges makes great semi-permanent soft-anarchy pieces.

Shown here is a selection of Antoni & Alison badge designs. "We made badges as souvenirs of our ideas – so we could give them away and 'spread the word'," says Burakowski. "Unfortunately that's why we don't have any left."

www.antoniandalison.co.uk

Souvenir for the year 2000

7p

QUACK QUACK

boring, boring, boring, boring

ANTONI ALISON

Love it.

VISIONARY.

GIN + TONIC

POPULAR MUSEUM SOUVENIRS

ANTONI ALISON

POPULAR FACTORY OF LIGHTS & EXPERIMENT

i Love WINK-Y

A★A Go

DAmN it.

WEAR ME BE NAKED

DDD... IIII SSSS CCCC

REALLY Boring / Boring

I CAN FLY

A★A Do

LADY LUCK RULES OK

Leona Baker started her jewellery label in February 2003, calling it Lady Luck after her boyfriend gave her the nickname when she kept returning from car-boot sales with loads of pretty vintage things. A random find at one such sale led to the creation of a range of jewellery made from old rock badges. "It was on one of my lucky trips to the Bank Holiday Wimbledon car-boot sale that I came across a tatty cardboard box of acrylic band badges," Baker explains. "The box included Thin Lizzy, Mick Jagger, Toyah, AC/DC, Duran Duran, Culture Club, Joan Jett, Led Zeppelin, Status Quo and Go-Go's badges, as well as Sex Pistols and AC/DC stickers."

The rest, as they say, is history. Baker changed her label's name to Lady Luck Rules OK (in order to dissociate it from a National Lottery ad campaign in the UK) and continued to salvage what badges she could, bought a drill and some leather to back them with, and began making them into earrings. Initially selling them from her stall at Portobello Market in London, the jewellery garnered interest from magazines such as *The Face*, *Sleazenation* and *Kerrang!*. Not only that, but the popularity of her badge-jewellery has seen her wholesale the collection to independent boutiques across the UK and Iceland, Hong Kong, Japan and the US.

www.ladyluckrulesok.com

STEFFEN ULLMANN

Berlin-based image-maker Steffen Ullmann makes badges and sells them on his website. Just for fun.

www.00v00.de

ANNA-OM-LINE

Galicia-based interactive and multimedia designer Anna Maria Lopez Lopez works under the moniker anna-OM-Line and is the design director for Spain's Crafts & Design Council. Here is a selection of her badges commemorating her digital artwork – all are available from dedicated button-badge site Prickie.com (see page 94).

www.anna-OM-line.com

BORIS DWORSCHAK

A graphic and type designer living in Germany, Boris Dworschak has created several typefaces for Die Gestalten Verlag and released some, such as Gaijin and Raster, through foundry T.26. Here are some badges he has designed.

www.borisdworschak.de

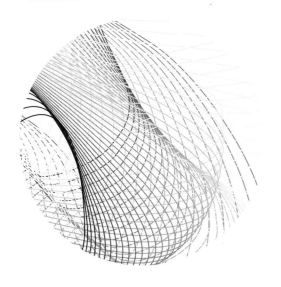

INTERCITY

London-based graphic design studio Intercity comprises the talents of Nick Foot, Nathan Gale and Tu Hoang. Founded in 2004, the company has produced editorial, web, illustration and identity work for a variety of clients including 55DSL, Bush Records, Carhartt, *Creative Review*, HMV, *MacUser* and Topshop.

"We first got into badge design after being asked to contribute to Stereohype's second By Invitation Only badge collection [see page 98]," explains Gale. "Creating badges quickly becomes addictive as they are a great place to instantly realize ideas or recycle elements of previous or unused work."

www.intercitydesign.com

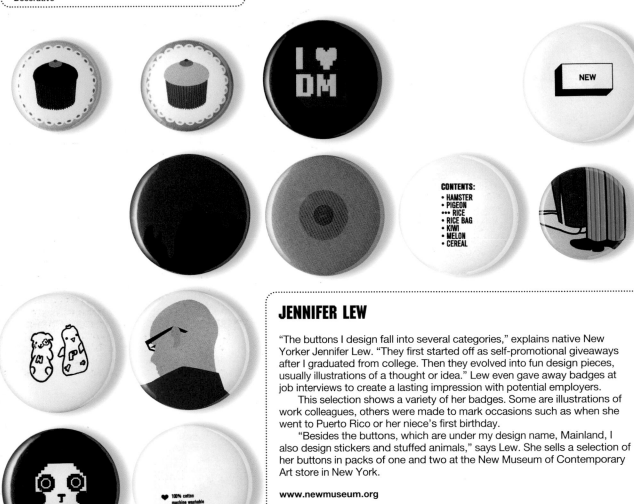

JENNIFER LEW

"The buttons I design fall into several categories," explains native New Yorker Jennifer Lew. "They first started off as self-promotional giveaways after I graduated from college. Then they evolved into fun design pieces, usually illustrations of a thought or idea." Lew even gave away badges at job interviews to create a lasting impression with potential employers.

This selection shows a variety of her badges. Some are illustrations of work colleagues, others were made to mark occasions such as when she went to Puerto Rico or her niece's first birthday.

"Besides the buttons, which are under my design name, Mainland, I also design stickers and stuffed animals," says Lew. She sells a selection of her buttons in packs of one and two at the New Museum of Contemporary Art store in New York.

www.newmuseum.org

ROSE + SADIE

Graphic designer Tracy White and philosophy graduate Carly Stair produce pin badges in San Francisco under the name Rose + Sadie. Their badges are notably not plastic-coated but instead for the most part consist of felt illustrations stitched onto fabric, which are then stretched round the badge in the usual way.

"We started making pins for fun and for friends," explains White. However, once the pair started selling their creations in a shop in San Francisco, they saw greater possibilities. Now their pins are stocked in more than a dozen stores across the US. "We don't really have any big plans," they say, "as long as we continue having fun doing it. Plus, we do have day jobs!"

www.roseandsadie.com

EBOY

The Berlin- and New York-based graphics studio known simply as eBoy hardly needs an introduction. Its championing of pixel graphics is world famous (its style is often imitated) and its members admit to finding inspiration in video games, commercials, Lego and other trappings of Western culture. In 2006 they produced a selection of colourful, unmistakeably eBoy button badges to sell through dedicated badge website Prickie.com (see page 94). Explore the wonderful world of eBoy on its website – but first check out these badges…

www.eboy.com

PESKIMO

Peskimo is the name given to the combined creative output of Jodie and David, two monster-loving designers who specialize in character creation, illustration and animation. The pair have worked on projects for clients such as CBBC, *Computer Arts*, *Digital Creative Arts*, Mimoco, MTV, NoStore, Play Imaginative and Sony PSP. They have also exhibited work and have products for sale around the world. In addition, they host a very jolly website that's worth exploring as it shows much of their work to date and has games to play and stuff to download. Here we see a selection of some of the numerous badges they've produced, including some ingeniously packaged in heart-shaped origami creations. Peskimo has also contributed badge designs to Pinpops.com (see page 104) and also to Stereohype's By Invitation Only badge project (see page 98).

www.peskimo.com

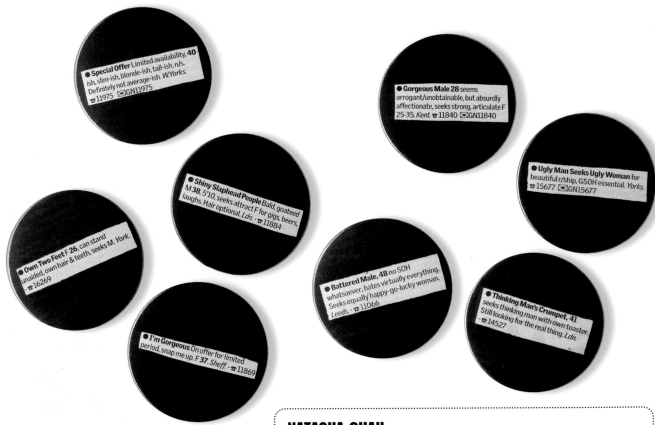

● **Special Offer** Limited availability, **40**-ish, slim-ish, blonde-ish, tall-ish, n/s. Definitely not average-ish. *W.Yorks.* ☎11975 ✉GN11975

● **Gorgeous Male 28** seems arrogant/unobtainable, but absurdly affectionate, seeks strong, articulate F 25-35. *Kent.* ☎11840 ✉GN11840

● **Ugly Man Seeks Ugly Woman** for beautiful r/ship, GSOH essential. *Yorks.* ☎15677 ✉GN15677

● **Shiny Slaphead People** Bald, goateed M **38**, 5'10, seeks attract F for gigs, beers, laughs. Hair optional. *Ldn.* - ☎11884

● **Own Two Feet** F **26**, can stand unaided, own hair & teeth, seeks M. *York.* - ☎16269

● **Battered Male, 48** no SOH whatsoever, hates virtually everything. Seeks equally happy-go-lucky woman. *Leeds.* - ☎11066

● **Thinking Man's Crumpet, 41** Still looking for the real thing. *Ldn.* - ☎14527 seeks thinking man with own toaster.

● **I'm Gorgeous** On offer for limited period, snap me up. F **37**. *Sheff.* - ☎11869

● **Life's Too Short** to dance with ugly men when you can be with a chilled black **30** something F. *Mancs.* - ☎13208

NATASHA SHAH

Natasha Shah graduated from the London College of Printing with a BA in Graphic Design and Media in 2003. After stints at Design Machine in New York and Exposure in London, she set up as a freelance designer in late 2005. Shown here are badges from her Lonely Arts badge project. All are made from real singles ads cut from newspapers.

"What's great about singles ads is that, without a picture, people have to get across in as few words as possible what they're like," observes Shah. "They have to be creative to stand out on a crowded page and have to inject their personality and characteristics in such a way that the ad will attract the right kind of person. No mean feat. These badges represent just a handful of ads that I think have perfected the art."

www.natashashah.co.uk
nat@natashashah.co.uk

NATHAN FLETCHER

Nathan Fletcher is an illustrator based in the southwest of the UK.

This series of badges was commissioned by dedicated badge website Pinpops.com (see page 104). Fletcher responded to an open brief by offering up his take on the traditional horror characters of Dracula, Frankenstein's Monster and a mummy. "I was trying to play around with how you feel about these characters," he explains. "Although they are obviously 'nasty', you tend to feel some sort of affection towards them."

www.mybrokenshoe.com

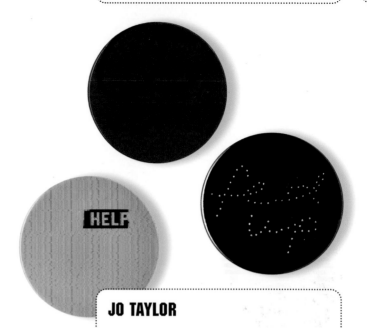

JO TAYLOR

These badges are from a series of 24 which formed part of a research project by Jo Taylor when she was at London's Royal College of Art.

She explains: "The aim of this project, which was called See You Later, was to bring creativity and delight into communication with older people. The badges were exhibited at the RCA in 2002 as part of an installation that included a sound piece, wall drawing and slideshow and they were used in a series of presentations to young designers to provoke thinking and discussion."

www.arcolacollective.com
www.thisisjo.com

G THE P

G the P is the DJ name of a certain Gavin Lucas, the author of this rather splendid book. It's also the name under which he creates badges – just for the fun of it. Badges for badges' sake. Shown here is a set of four badges inspired by a tea towel owned by an ex-flatmate that displayed the International Flag Code in its colourful glory. Each flag in the code represents a letter of the alphabet and also has its own specific meaning. Applying the code to these badges, the half-blue, half-yellow one means "I wish to communicate with you", while the yellow badge with the thick blue stripe translates as "I'm manoeuvring with difficulty".

The other badges shown here are part of an ongoing typographic project. Each badge utilizes a different typeface and was designed specifically for one of the maker's friends. At the time of writing, there is a plan afoot for G the P and Intercity (see page 23) to join forces and produce limited-edition badge sets under the moniker Badge/Button/Pin.

www.myspace.com/gthep

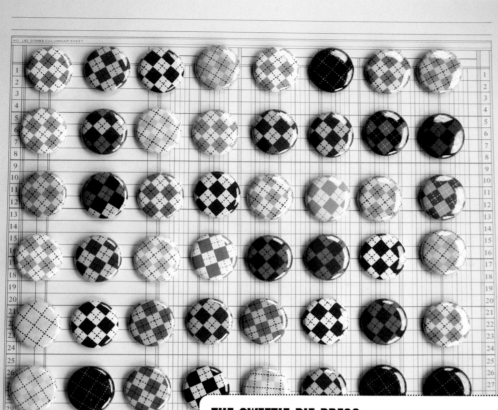

THE SWEETIE PIE PRESS

"The Sweetie Pie Press started out as a loose, anarchic zine publishing endeavour," explains founder Becky Johnson. Johnson publishes zines and creates badges with various artist friends, and the work is documented on the Sweetie Pie Press website. Series of Badges she's commissioned include the Lovely Ladies With Awkward Instruments series by Reverend Aitor, the Country Greats series by Ehren Salazar and the Unpopular Vegetables series by Emma Segal. We particularly like her exploration of different colourways of the classic argyle pattern.

www.sweetiepiepress.com

JUDITH EGGER

These jolly designs are by Munich-based performance and installation artist Judith Egger. As well as creating and exhibiting installations, she runs the experimental music/art label Edition Graphon.

"I'm fascinated by the never-ending possibilities of this minimal showcase," she says of badges. "Wearing a badge, you can present an idea, provoke, make someone laugh, think or make a political statement."

www.judithegger.com
www.editiongraphon.com

JOHANNES BREYER

Johannes Breyer of Buckenhof in Germany sent an envelope of colourful, illustrated badges in response to the call for entries for this book. An email address appeared on the envelope but Breyer didn't respond to our messages of thanks. All we can tell you is that we really like his badges and the hand-drawn envelope they arrived in – which we have also included here.

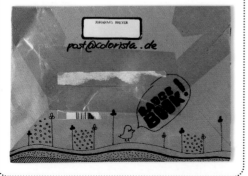

NEENOON

Los Angeles-based Ben and Reneé Loiz started NeeNoon in 2002. "It began as a way for us to work together creating products that we enjoy making," they explain. "After years of creating items for ourselves, friends and exhibitions, we decided to open the NeeNoon shop – a place where we could make these items available to anyone interested."

These badges were made as accessories for the NeeNoon autumn/winter 2004 clothing range.

www.neenoon.com
www.typevsm.com
www.reneeloiz.com

TAKESHI HAMADA

Tiger is the name of Takeshi Hamada's online magazine that showcases illustration, poetry, photography, art and news about upcoming exhibitions and workshops – all from a number of contributors from around the world. Hamada has reproduced some of the best work from Tigermagazine.org as well as some of his own work (such as the "busy" tiger shown top left) in badge form.

www.tigermagazine.org

PROMO-
TIONAL

™

BUILD

Michael C. Place of London-based design studio Build is one of the UK's most respected graphic designers. He has produced badges for a range of projects including Pinpops.com (see page 104), Oneinchlove.com (see page 122) and Wearitwithpride.com (see page 88). Here are just a few of the badges he has designed in the last few years.

www.designbybuild.com

XL RECORDINGS

In the lead-up to Christmas in 2003 and 2004 greetings cards were sent out to clients by internationally renowned record label XL Recordings. Each card featured a selection of badges with either text or design relating specifically to one of the label's acts, which include Basement Jaxx, Dizzee Rascal, M.I.A. and The White Stripes, to name but a few. The label regularly produces badges for its bands, a selection of which are also shown here.

www.xlrecordings.com

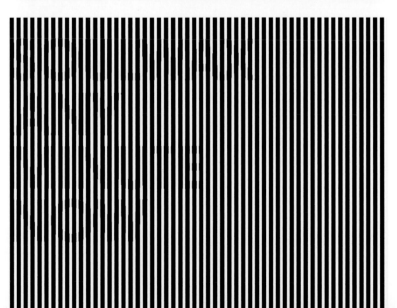

SOULWAX BADGES

Musician, DJ and designer Trevor Jackson created the black-and-white artwork for Soulwax's third album and the singles and posters promoting it. Varying thicknesses in what first appear to be a regular white pattern on black ground create text that seems to lurk behind the image. Best not to stare too long – just long enough to glimpse what's written through the stripes on the sleeve of single Any Minute Now (bottom left); the dots on the sleeve of the album of the same name (top); and the concentric rings of single E Talking. The artwork carried through to two promotional badges that came out too – although no amount of staring reveals any text: one badge has black-and-white stripes, the other is black with white dots.

www.trevorjackson.org

IT'S BIGGER THAN

It's Bigger Than is a monthly London party conceived and organized by a collective of enthusiastic DJs and designer James Joyce of One Fine Day. Joyce not only created a logo for the club night but also undertook the task of creating a bespoke illustration for each flyer promoting the events. At each party, badges commemorating the relevant flyer's design are handed out to further celebrate the artwork and promote It's Bigger Than.

At the first birthday of the club night, Joyce produced a series of hand-drawn, one-off badges, including his 1♥ design that was later redrawn and featured in a project Joyce completed for Carhartt clothing.

www.one-fine-day.co.uk
www.itsbiggerthan.com

GBH MAILER FOR D&AD

London design company GBH created this badge-tastic mailer for D&AD education initiative The Clinic back in 2001. The mail-out was sent to 40 design and advertising creatives chosen to participate in The Clinic, a project in which industry professionals hooked up with "partners" at designated colleges and offered them benefits such as placements, sponsorships, visiting lectureships, project-setting/critting, etc.

www.gregorybonnerhale.com
www.dandad.org

Congratulations. You're in a very privileged position. You are one of just forty leading design or advertising creatives chosen to represent your company at D&AD's newest Education initiative: The Clinic.

As you know, nothing is more important to D&AD than its commitment to education and that is why we've created a special event which links you and your design or advertising agency with a number of the country's leading colleges, ensuring education benefits from industry and industry connects with education.

Your commitment is a fifteen minute meeting with each of your designated College 'partners', during which you decide exactly which of your benefits you are prepared to offer. Benefits can range from placements, sponsorship, visiting lectures, setting and critting a project or even inventing your own special commitment, all helping your college to aim higher. Go on, promise the earth!

STUPID LOVE

Buenos Aires-based Virginia Christe and Federico Paltrinieria work together on motion-graphics and web-design projects as well as character design and illustration. Stupid Love is, in their own words, "our personal art project".

"At the moment we are not selling our badges as we make them as promotional items to give away," they maintain. "But we are thinking of a way to offer them to a buying public. Most likely in packs of four, each with an original handmade piece of artwork forming the main part of the packaging."

www.st-love.com.ar

AIR STUDIO

Air Studio in Milan comprises the talents of Franco Brambilla, Alessandro Cavallini, Pierluigi Longo, Alfio Mazzei, Simona Pinto and Giacomo Spazio. The badges shown here were created in 2004 by Cavallini, Pinto and Spazio for self-promotional purposes.

www.spazio.org/airstudio

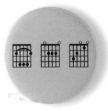

KIM JONES

Since graduating from the Central St Martins MA Menswear course with a distinction in 2001, designer Kim Jones has developed a cult following for his refined casual clothing. Alongside his own collection, Jones designs and works for a variety of companies, perhaps most notably Umbro, for whom he produces a range entitled Umbro by Kim Jones.

    Shown here are some badges Jones has designed for clients *Dazed and Confused,* Umbro and Topman.

www.kimjones.com

COLETTE

Über-cool Paris store Colette produces badges at the drop of a hat. Never sold but rather given away at events, parties or in-store, the badges are designed by Colette's creative director Sarah, regular Colette collaborators Kuntzel & Deygas (who famously created the brilliant animated title sequence for the film *Catch Me If You Can*), or by the likes of SO_ME or Genevieve Gauckler.

www.colette.fr

KAREN JANE

London graphic designer Karen Jane's Great Badge-Away project saw her give dozens of badges away free to people who looked at her website in the summer of 2005. "The idea behind it was mostly to make contact with people who casually passed through my site," she explains. First Karen designed a selection of badges, then built a page for her website which contained email-launching mouse-over buttons so that visitors to the site could select a badge and email her without undue effort to let her know their choice of design. Over the months following the launch, Karen sent out almost 100 badges to destinations as far-flung as America, Australia and Singapore, as well as to Holland, Finland, Portugal, France and the UK. Many happy recipients, such as Jeff Metal (shown), sent back images of themselves wearing their free badge. Karen also created this special d-pin font for the project. The letter shapes are based on the metal pin part used to make a one-inch badge.

www.karenjane.com

REGGAE ALLSTARS

30 BADGES TO COLLECT!

... Perry, Marcia Griffiths, Michael Rose

REGGAE ALLSTARS

30 BADGES TO COLLECT!

IN THIS PACK Jimmy Cliff, Admiral Baile, Althea & Donna

REGGAE ALLSTARS

30 BADGES TO COLLECT!

IN THIS PACK Augustus Pablo, Big Youth, Bob Marley

...E ALLST...

30 BADGE...

IN THIS PACK Ken...

★REGGAE★ ALLSTARS

30 BADGES TO COLLECT!

... Jerry, Coxsone Dodd, Prince Buster

★REGGAE★ ALLSTARS

30 BADGES TO COLLECT!

IN THIS PACK John Holt, Junior Delgado, Junior Murvin

★REGGAE★ ALLSTARS

30 BADGES TO COLLECT!

IN THIS PACK Peter Tosh, Susan Cadogan, Prince Jazzbo

...E ALLS...

30 BAD...

IN THIS PACK Briga...

ADMIRAL BAILE — ALTHEA & DONNA — AUGUSTUS PABLO — BIG YOUTH — BOB MARLEY — BRIGADIER JERRY — CLEMENT DODD — PRINCE BUSTER — DENNIS BROWN — DENNIS ALCAPONE — DILLINGER — GREGORY ISSACS — I-ROY

JAH WOOSH — JOHN HOLT — JUNIOR DELGADO — JUNIOR MURVIN — KEN BOOTHE — KING STITT — KING TUBBY — "SCRATCH" PERRY — MARCIA GRIFFITHS — MICHAEL ROSE — PETER TOSH — SUSAN CADOGAN — PRINCE JAZZBO

★REGGAE★ ALLSTARS

PHIL PRATT — U-ROY — HORACE ANDY — JIMMY CLIFF

NEW

NEW

London-based illustration, design and art-direction duo NEW comprises the talents of Austin Cowdall and Matt Hamilton.

In 2004 they created Reggae Allstars, a series of illustrations of the pair's favourite 30 Jamaican recording artists which manifested itself in a Dingbat typeface and also a series of badges made available online in ten packs of four badges. Each pack contained three different reggae stars and a NEW badge.

"Reggae Allstars is really our illustrated guide to original reggae stars whose music pretty much everyone has heard at some time or another at parties, festivals, carnivals, on TV, in clubs, bars, towerblocks, cars," explains Cowdall. "We scanned long-forgotten roots/reggae sleeves and press articles from the 1960s to the 1980s in search of visual references for our own personal favourite top-30 Jamaican recording artists and this is the result: a typeface, poster, T-shirt and badges you can buy online!"

www.NEW-online.co.uk

KENZO MINAMI

Apart from his commercial work as an art director/designer, New York-based Kenzo Minami is highly sought after for his paintings and digital artworks. He started his own clothing company in the spring of 2004 and promptly created some black-and-white badges as part of a promotional pack housed in a clear plastic DVD case. Kenzo Minami is represented internationally by the CWC Group.

www.kenzominami.com
www.cwctokyo.com (Asia)
www.cwc-i.com (United States and Europe)

LEMON JELLY

Lemon Jelly is as much known for the beautiful artwork that adorns its record sleeves as for its music thanks to its continuing collaboration with Airside (see page 85). The connection between band and design agency: co-founder of Airside Fred Deakin is also in Lemon Jelly.

This set of nine badges was created to promote Lemon Jelly's album '64–'95, which was released in January 2005. Each badge displays artwork created for the album, which was released on vinyl, CD and also as a DVD, a film having been made to accompany each audio track.

www.lemonjelly.ky

JEREMYVILLE

Jeremyville is based in Sydney, Australia. He designs toys and books, paints murals, writes newspaper columns, creates animation, produces his Jeremyville clothing label, and runs a growing online store. With Megan Mair, he also designed and produced the world's first book dedicated to designer toys called *Vinyl Will Kill!*, published by IdN. Recent design and illustration clients have included Adio footwear, the musician Beck, Coca-Cola, Diesel, 55DSL, MTV and X-Box. Jeremyville products are stocked in stores including Colette in Paris (see page 47). Perhaps unsurprisingly, among the myriad products and goodies he produces are these lavishly printed (some on silver paper) badges, each one individually packaged.

www.jeremyville.com

FEMKE HIEMSTRA

Illustrator and artist Femke Hiemstra lives and works in Amsterdam, Holland. Her artworks are created using a mixture of collage, acrylic paints, pencil, chalk, wood, clay and marker pens. Her illustration work, on the other hand, demonstrates her love of character design and tends to combine traditional hand-drawing techniques with the software packages Photoshop and Illustrator. She's been making badges since 2003 and they can be bought at Dutch website Buzzworks.com (see page 92).

"I use the canvas of the badge as a miniature playground for my ideas and characters," says Hiemstra. "It's a great relief to have something like that to do in between jobs for clients. And seeing other fans of cute and cuddly merchandise wearing your buttons makes a gloomy day bright!"

www.femtasia.nl

Leave No **CEO** Behind

SECRECY Promotes Tyranny

W A R

SURVEILLANCE Undermines Liberty

DISSENT Protects Democracy

Preemptive **WAR** Is Terrorism

I ♥ NY

'W' STANDS FOR WRONG

'W' WRONG ON JOBS

'W' WRONG ON CIVIL LIBERTIES

'W' WRONG ON WOMEN'S RIGHTS

'W' WRONG ON THE WAR

'W' WRONG ON EDUCATION

MILTON GLASER

Perhaps the most prolific and best-known American graphic designer of modern times, Milton Glaser is no stranger to button-badge design. Shown on this page are two sets of buttons he designed in 2003 for *The Nation* magazine. The bottom six form the Nation Dubya Set while the six at the top form the less imaginatively titled, but no less politically terse, Six Button Set. Also shown here is a badge with Glaser's now iconic I♥NY design. On the following spread are two further (more recent) sets of buttons Glaser has designed for *The Nation*.

www.miltonglaser.com

The Nation Button Initiative

Do the Right Thing

The midterm elections will decide our future.

The Red and The Black, 6 Button Set, $15, available at www.thenation.com

Actual size is 1.25 inches in diameter.

The Nation Button Initiative

It's time for Reds and Blues to put principles above politics.

"The Purple Coalition" 9 Button Set, $20, available at www.thenation.com

PARRA

Amsterdam-based Parra, aka Pieter Janssen, has produced illustrations and posters for clients such as Ben & Jerry's, Footlocker and, more recently, the Samaritans. He's designed a shoe for Nike and his style is instantly recognizable: hand-drawn typography, beautiful use of flat, vibrant colours and the occasional inclusion of strange creatures.

In 2000 Parra set up a skate clothing label, Rockwell Clothing, which produces items that feature his graphics. Most of the badges shown on these pages promote the label and are just some of the myriad badge designs that were available to buy at his first UK solo exhibition entitled *Jobs I Do For Friends For Less Than £100* which ran at London's Kemistry Gallery in early 2005.

www.rockwellclothing.com

HOUSE 33

The House 33 store (which is sadly no more) in London's Soho was the brainchild of Delaware font design shop House Industries, designer Jeremy Dean and fashion-trend forecaster and designer Simon "Barnzley" Armitage. It sold three exclusive brands, House, 33 and House 33, with the aim of "bringing the best of illustration and graphic design into the fashion world". Ken Barber, Andy Cruz and Jeremy Dean designed this selection of buttons which could be picked up on the counter in the shop to serve as a memento of one's visit. While soaring Soho rents have meant the physical shop has gone, House 33 products are still available from the House 33 website.

www.house33.com

PACKS

CHRIS BETTIG

Chris Bettig is the founder of The Mountain Label – in his own words, "a multi-disciplinary design, production and art-direction company which has designed interiors and displays for the likes of Urban Outfitters and Nike". The Mountain Label also has a small range of products and clothing which are sold through select retailers.

These buttons were produced essentially as self-promotional items to be sold at solo exhibitions in Bettig's hometown of Los Angeles. The two-colour badge pack promotes his clothing and accessory line.

www.themountainlabel.com

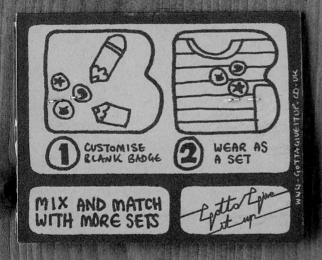

GEORGE WU/ GOTTA GIVE IT UP

"My love of badges seems to stem from birthday parties," reveals graphic designer George Wu. "You knew you were important on that day because of your enormous badge!" Wu creates packs of badges under the name Gotta Give It Up, including these Badger packs, which feature badger characters and also a blank speech-bubble badge in each set of three. "The idea with these is that the badges are worn together with a narrative spreading over a number of badges," explains Wu. "The wearer can also customize the story by completing the third badge. In the future I hope that there will be a whole world of Badger badge sets to mix and match and eventually the sets will include stickers which can be used to personalize the badges as well."

www.mywu.co.uk
george@mywu.co.uk

NEAL WHITTINGTON/ PRESENT AND CORRECT

Inspired by the *Boys Who Sew* exhibition at London's Crafts Council in early 2004, graphic designer Neal Whittington started making cross-stitch badges in his Tufnell Park flat, under the name Present and Correct. "I made a cross-stitch Scrabble letter badge for my friend's birthday and my friends said I should sell them." And sell them he did – and still does – in shops such as Best, Beyond the Valley, Magma, Tatty Devine and even on a market stall. "I like producing something so common but with a little twist to it," says Whittington. "And the craft thing is having a real resurgence. I try to put as much as I can into the packaging too, to get some witty copy in there. To make people smile."

www.presentandcorrect.com
info@presentandcorrect.com

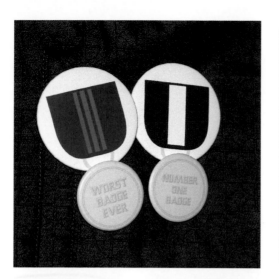

PETER MICHAEL WILLER

Danish graphics student Peter Michael Willer became interested in badges when studying at the London College of Printing in 2003. He created his first badge pack, Law & Order Roleplay, in 2004. This contained four badges with an interrogation room role on each – Good Cop, Bad Cop, 100% Guilty and Not Guilty. Also shown are his Home Office Badge Statistics, Fashion Statements, Law & Order Nicknames and Medal badge sets.

petermw@dgh.dk

istmas

EW YEAR!

FELT ANIMAL BADGES

Decorate Clothes or Furnishings

PESTS

MARK PAWSON

London-based artist and collector of "essential ephemera" Mark Pawson has been making badges for around 20 years. His badges tend to be packaged in sets of four "to make them more presentable" and these packs usually contain bonus stickers. Some are based around a slogan theme, others are made up of found symbols or icons, while still more feature patterns found on the insides of envelopes or Japanese origami paper. The latter represent, he says, "a move towards making badges more like jewellery, more decorative". If it contained no work by Mark Pawson, the present volume would be like a book on Italian Renaissance art that makes no mention of Leonardo da Vinci.

www.mpawson.demon.co.uk

yClipArt
eSet

Edition)

AngryClipArt
BadgeSet

(ScribbleEdition)

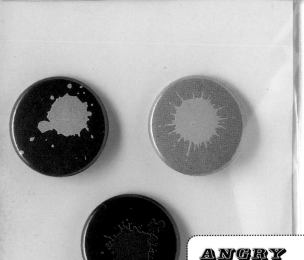

ANGRY

Angry is the fashion and product-design arm of Dublin-based company Aad. While Aad produces design work for a range of corporate and arts clients, Angry creates ranges of T-shirts, clothing and badge packs and adds new products to its website every month. The badge packs each contain three or four badges which playfully reference Angry's graphic-design roots.

www.angryretail.com

2006
gryretail.com
udioaad.com

**AngryBadges
No.002**

AngryFonts
BadgeSet

(DisplayEdition)

©Angry2006
www.angryretail.com
www.studioaad.com

AngryBadges
No.003

AngryRabbits
BadgeSet

(ParklifeEdition)

©Angry2006
www.angryretail.com
www.studioaad.com

An
No

BRUNFTZEIT

Brunftzeit (which means "mating season" in German) was set up in 2003 by Björn Asmussen and Carolin Enste as, they tell us, "a creative playground where we can design and publish badges, clothing and all kinds of accessories ranging from earrings to custom-made fabric dolls".

The pair have created a number of five-badge sets which come packaged unusually in fabric packs. Shown here are the Country and Sitzen (German for "sitting") sets.

www.brunftzeit.com

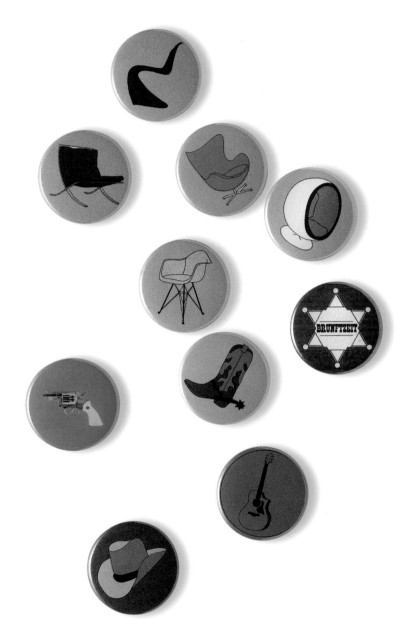

2000 MONTREAL G2Q
PROTEST SET
BY CHRIS BENTZEN

1997 UBC APEC
PROTEST SET
BY CHRIS BENTZEN

1999 SEATTE WTO
PROTEST SET
BY CHRIS BENTZEN

CHRIS BENTZEN

Shown here are three sets of three buttons produced by Chris Bentzen of Vancouver, each of which "commemorates notable protests in Canada". Contextual descriptions appear on the back of the card on which each set is mounted.

Bentzen's love of button badges doesn't stop with making them. Together with fellow enthusiast Jim Hoehnle, he runs the annual Vancouver button-badge event Hot One-Inch Action. Since 2004, the one-night-only happening has been bringing together the work of 50 artists, all presented on one-inch buttons displayed on the exhibition space's walls. Attendees can buy a bag of five randomly selected badges from the show. If they want a particular badge they are encouraged to trade with the other attendees. To help encourage this, beverages, live music and DJs are thrown into the festive mix.

The event has been a roaring success and has even inspired a similar event in Toronto called One-Inch Punch (www.lesrobots.ca/oneinchpunch.html).

http://buttons.thisisplanb.net
buttons@thisisplanb.net

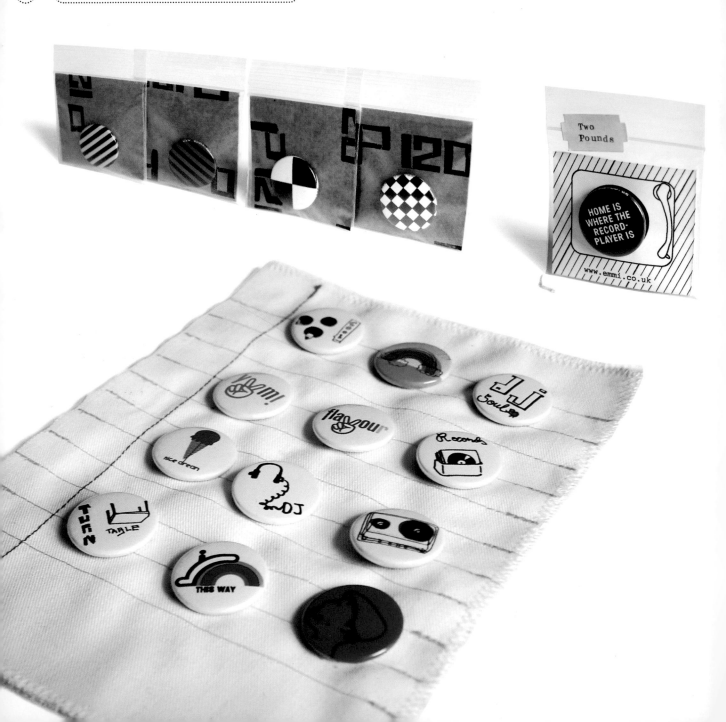

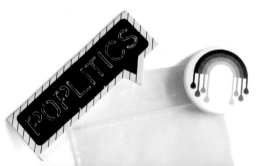

EMMI SALONEN

Finnish-born graphic designer Emmi Salonen is a prolific badge-maker, sometimes producing them as decorative, jewellery-like accessories and sometimes as political or personal statements.

"I produce and design badges because it's like making a present for a friend," she reveals. "The first ones I ever made were part of a series entitled News Icon in 2001, which were designed to bring awareness of current affairs to young people. Proper, traditional political agitation! From there I've carried on making political badge graphics or just decorating people's bags and shirts with one-inch shapes and colours that I find intriguing. Often I also design special packaging that reflects the theme of the badges I make."

www.emmi.co.uk

**Andrew
Rae**

2

collection two

Concrete Hermit Consumer Products

**Concrete
Hermit**

1

collection one

CONCRETE HERMIT

Founder Chris Knight explains: "Concrete Hermit was started in 2004 as a way for designers and artists to realize their ideas for T-shirt designs without having to face prohibitive start-up costs. Many of our designs are produced in strictly limited editions so you can be assured of an individual product not to be found anywhere else. We have rapidly expanded to produce badges and now stock a range of books."

Artists who have already produced badge sets for Concrete Hermit include John Allcott, Phil Ashcroft (Phlash), Jon Burgerman, DataSelected, Kate Moross, Andrew Rae and Ian Stevenson (I Like Drawing).

www.concretehermit.com

ALEXANDER GELMAN

Alexander Gelman, founder of Design Machine in New York, loves buttons. For the past five years he has been commemorating his graphic-design projects by miniaturizing them to fit onto one-inch buttons. They come in sets of three, lavishly housed in die-cut and foil-blocked card packs, which effectively raises the status of the humble button to that of must-have accessory and art object.

www.glmn.com

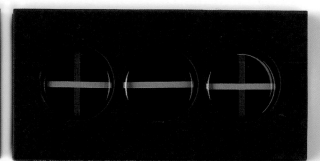

Not for children! The Gohann Collection
Limited Edition Artist's Buttons

Set: 555 Machine
Ambient Art Nothing
30.00 usd Dim O.O.
30.00 eu Clmn Something
19.00 gbp Impact Subtraction
3,588 jpy Infiltrate

2003 © A. Gohaun. All rights reserved.

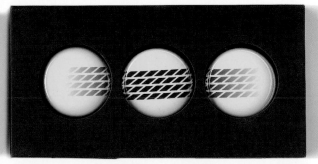

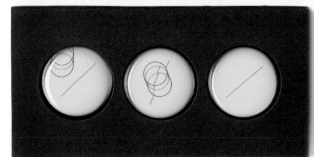

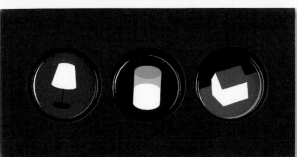

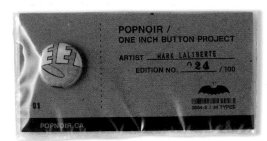

POP NOIR

Pop Noir is an ongoing project by Toronto-based artist Mark Laliberte. In his own words, "The umbrella term 'Pop Noir' is a catchphrase, a curatorial concern, an involvement strategy. I am using it to define the residue of my own aesthetic, an aesthetic based on fusing oppositions and on synthesizing unharmonious parts."

The Pop Noir One-Inch Button Project is a series of 24 artist buttons, each released in an edition of 100, packaged on a numbered card sealed in plastic. Some of the badges, though, are one-offs, such as the fifth Pop Noir button release, 100 Heads. Here Toronto artist Balint Zsako created 100 original miniature images of heads using watercolours – rather than reproduce one image 100 times. To view an animation featuring all 100 Zsako heads, visit www.popnoir.ca/inch-05.html.

www.popnoir.ca
www.marklaliberte.com

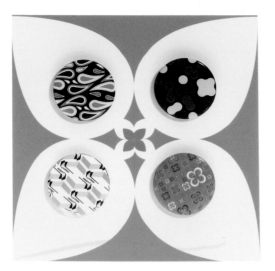

AIRSIDE

London-based design studio Airside was set up in 1999 by Alex Maclean, Fred Deakin and Nat Hunter. While producing work across the disciplines of moving image, graphic design, illustration and digital and interactive media for clients such as Coca-Cola, MTV and Orange, they also create products to sell through their online shop such as T-shirts, badges, vinyl and knitted toys, keyrings, posters, art prints… In short, the studio's creativity and productivity seems boundless.

Here are two packs of Airside badges available from Airsideshop.com – Patterns and Sayings. Also shown is the box set of Refugee.com pins. But it's not all about selling badges. Also shown here is a selection of badges made by Airside that were just lying about the studio.

www.airside.co.uk
www.airsideshop.com

WAYNE DALY

Graphic designer Wayne Daly created these Consumer Choice badges in 2003 in response to his love of price stickers. "I found myself with a growing collection of price stickers – I suppose my version of stamp collecting," he explains. "I felt I wanted to utilize them in some way, and selling the stickers on to other people seemed an ideal way of doing this. I became interested in investigating the idea of 'value' – what factors inform a person's decision when buying a product? The customer is presented with a range of badges, priced according to the value declared on the price stickers themselves."

From this project arose the 99p badge range which was produced exclusively for the Magma bookshop. "Magma liked the idea of the standard Consumer Choice badges but the irregular pricing of the range proved, understandably, to be overly complicated for their item-pricing system, hence the set price of 99p – a price that somehow always promises good value."

www.waynedaly.com

WEBSITES

WEAR IT WITH PRIDE

Darren Firth set up Wear It With Pride in 2003 and since then has tirelessly
rallied illustrators and graphic designers, persuading them to design
badges to be displayed and sold on the site. And he hasn't done badly at all
– his site now contains well over 170 badges by the likes of Jon Burgerman,
Büro Destruct, Dalek, Devil Robots, David Horvath, Insect, Pixel Surgeon,
and Michael C. Place/Build.

And people are logging on and buying them: Wear It With Pride
received well over 100,000 hits last year, demonstrating the current pulling
power of the badge.

www.wearitwithpride.com

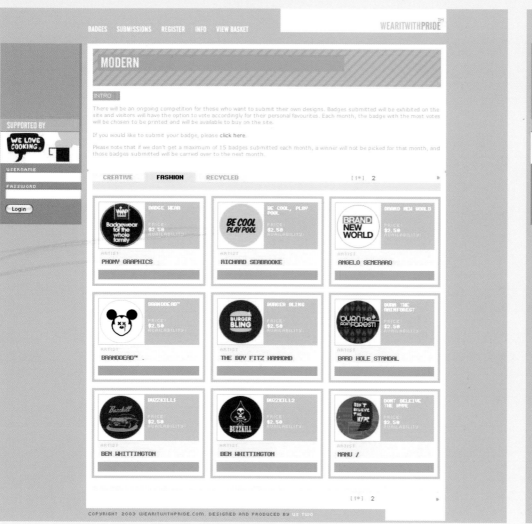

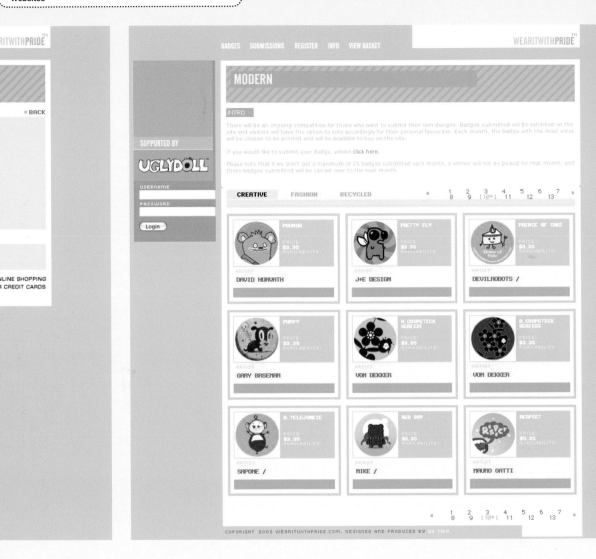

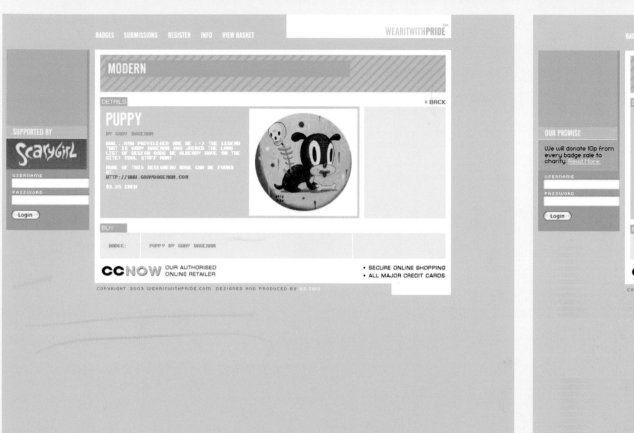

BUZZWORKS

Set up by Peter Giljam in 2000, Buzzworks is a Dutch website (designed by Like) that showcases and sells various cool, graphically adorned products, from printed T-shirts, vinyl toys and sew-on patches and beyond to skateboard decks and, of course, button badges. The site hosts a dedicated "button" section, on which hundreds of button badges – mostly designed by home-grown Dutch talent such as Delta, Parra (see page 60) and Femke Hiemstra (see page 56) – can be viewed and purchased. A must-visit online destination for the button-badge hungry!

www.buzzworks.nl
buzz@buzzworks.nl

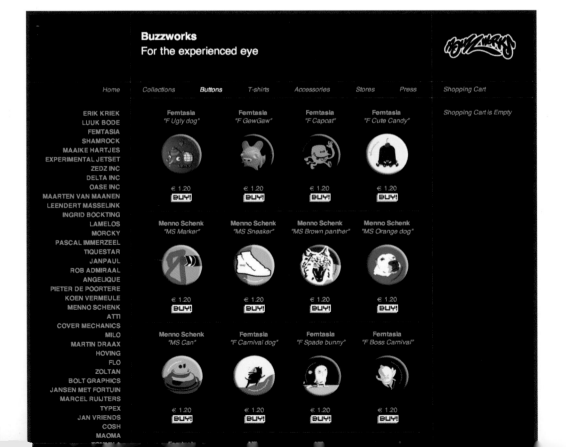

Luuk Bode
"LB Robogod"

€ 1.20
BUY!

Luuk Bode
"LB Devil orange"

€ 1.20
BUY!

Zware jongens
"ZW Wock"

€ 1.20
BUY!

Zware jongens
"ZJ I like HM"

€ 1.20
BUY!

Zware jongens
"ZW Disco will die"

€ 1.20
BUY!

Femtasia
"F Fempromo"

€ 1.20
BUY!

Shamrock
"S Redlight girl"

€ 1.20
BUY!

Shamrock
"S Girl talk"

€ 1.20
BUY!

Shamrock
"S Poison"

€ 1.20
BUY!

Shamrock
"S Shoes"

€ 1.20
BUY!

Shamrock
"S Nude"

€ 1.20
BUY!

Shamrock
"S Shamsterdam"

€ 1.20
BUY!

Shamrock
"S Disco"

€ 1.20
BUY!

Shamrock
"S Drunk"

€ 1.20
BUY!

Shamrock
"S Snotty Buzz"

€ 1.20
BUY!

Shamrock
"S Donkey pink"

€ 1.20
BUY!

Shamrock
"S Smokey"

€ 1.20
BUY!

Shamrock
"S Much bigger"

€ 1.20
BUY!

Shamrock
"S Friends"

€ 1.20
BUY!

Shamrock
"S Stinky"

€ 1.20
BUY!

Maaike Hartjes
"MH Happy bunny"

€ 1.20
BUY!

Shamrock
"S Sinterklaas"

€ 1.20
BUY!

Shamrock
"S Rabbit"

€ 1.20
BUY!

Shamrock
"S baby star"

€ 1.20
BUY!

PRICKIE

Prickie was launched in January 2006 by Eduardo Chavez and Peter Locke. The site is essentially an online gallery and shop for badges, browsable by artist. Anyone with badge designs can submit them (as long as they don't contain pornographic or copyright material), a concept that has proved remarkably popular: when the site first launched, the work of ten artists was displayed. By the end of the first six months, over 258 artists had submitted badge designs. At the time of writing, the site boasts over 5,000 badge designs. So do people actually buy the badges? "On average, we are getting ten orders a day," says Chavez. "The minimum order is three badges, but the average request is for about 20 badges for each order." All artists get a commission from sales and are free to set the price of their miniature masterpieces.

www.prickie.com

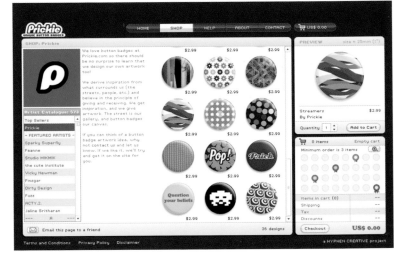

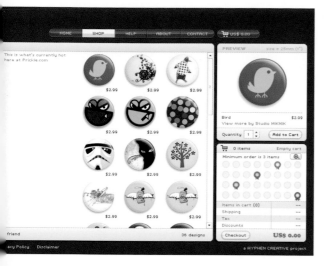

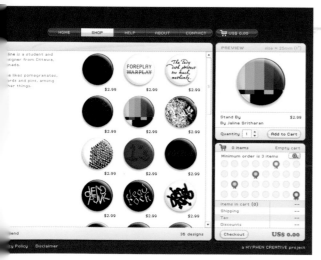

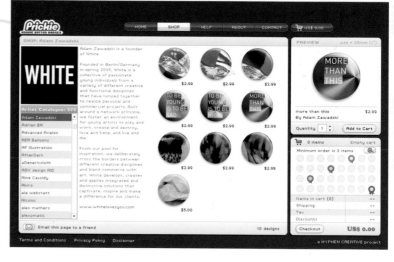

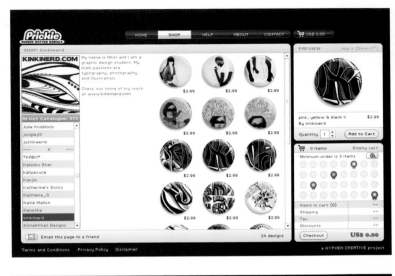

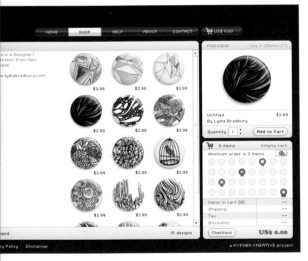

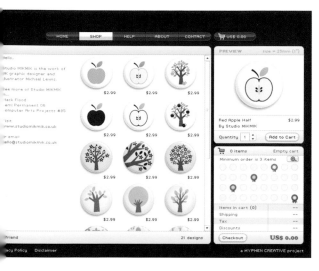

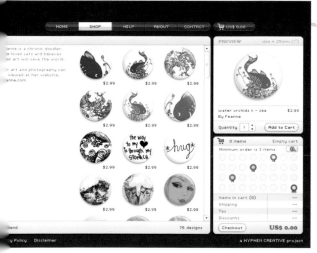

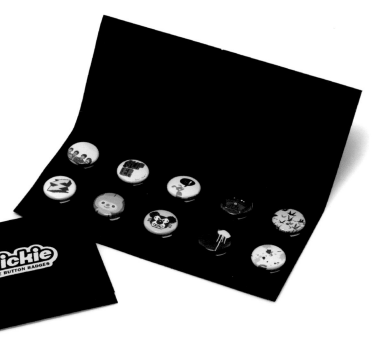

STEREOHYPE/
BY INVITATION ONLY

Launched in late 2004, Stereohype is the brainchild of Agathe Jacquillat and Tomi Vollauschek of FL@33. Showcasing products such as T-shirts and clothes made by them or fellow designers, it is described by the pair as "an online boutique offering limited editions and rare products that include exclusively commissioned artworks". Though not entirely dedicated to badges, Stereohype boasts the By Invitation Only (B.I.O.) badge initiative via which, every six months, FL@33 approach a selection of image-makers of their choice to produce a badge or series of badges. These are displayed in the B.I.O. section of the Stereohype site and can be purchased online. The ever-growing list of badge designers to get involved includes Jody Barton, Anthony Burrill, Deanne Cheuk, Patrick Duffy, Tom Gauld, Megumu Kasuga, Julian Morey, Vaughan Oliver, Michael C. Place/Build and Rinzen. B.I.O. undoubtedly makes Stereohype one of the coolest online shopping destinations for button badges.

www.stereohype.com

Stereohyne
graphic art & fashion boutique

    clothes · graphic art · products · info · view basket

quantity: 0   total: £0.00

B.I.O. series 2 **123klan** > £1.50 each/£5 set of 4 see their four badges	**B.I.O. series 2** **Adam Pointer** > £1.50 each/£5 set of 4 see his four badges	**B.I.O. series 2** **Birgit Simons** > £1.50 each/£5 set of 4 see her four badges	**B.I.O. series 2** **Dag Henning Brandsaeter** > £1.50 each/£4 set of 3 see his three badges
B.I.O. series 2 **Deanne Cheuk** > £1.50 each/£5 set of 4 see her four badges	**B.I.O. series 2** **Delaware** > £1.50 see details	**B.I.O. series 2** **FL@33** > £1.50 each/£5 set of 4 see their four badges	**B.I.O. series 2** **I love your t-shirt** > £1.50 each/£5 set of 4 see their four badges
B.I.O. series 2 **Intercity** > £1.50 each/£4 set of 3 see their three badges	**B.I.O. series 2** **Judith Egger** > £1.50 each/£5 set of 4 see her four badges	**B.I.O. series 2** **Julian Morey** > £1.50 each/£5 set of 4 see his four badges	**B.I.O. series 2** **Matthias & Helen** > £1.50 each/£5 set of 4 see their four badges
B.I.O. series 2 **onepom** > £1.50 each/£5 set of 4 see her four badges	**B.I.O. series 2** **Rinzen** > £1.50 each/£5 set of 4 see their four badges	**B.I.O. series 2** **Roderick Mills** > £1.50 each/£5 set of 4 see his four badges	**B.I.O. series 2** **Tom Skipp** > £1.50 each/£5 set of 4 see his four badges
B.I.O. series 2 **Wig-01** > £1.50 each/£5 set of 4 see his four badges	 **B.I.O.** (by invitation only) **button badge series 1** **SEE ALL 43 OF THEM**	**B.I.O.** (by invitation only) **button badge series 3** **SEE ALL 58 OF THEM**	**B.I.O.** (by invitation only) **button badge series 4** / NEW! **SEE ALL 41 OF THEM**
Competition Winners 2004 & 2005 **SEE ALL 20 OF THEM**			

 clothes · graphic art · products · info · view basket

quantity: 0   total: £0.00

B.I.O. series 3 **Basher** > £1.50 each/£5 set of 4 see his four badges	**B.I.O. series 3** **Brighten The Corners** > £1.50 each/£5 set of 4 see their four badges	**B.I.O. series 3** **Chosil Jan Kil** > £1.50 each/£5 set of 4 see her four badges	**B.I.O. series 3** **David Poldvari** > £1.50 each/£5 set of 4 see his four badges
B.I.O. series 3 **FL@33** > £1.50 each/£4 set of 3 see their three badges	**B.I.O. series 3** **French** > £1.50 each/£5 set of 4 see his four badges	**B.I.O. series 3** **Inksurge** > £1.50 each/£5 set of 4 see their four badges	**B.I.O. series 3** **Karen Jane** > £1.50 see details
B.I.O. series 3 **Luke Best** > £1.50 each/£5 set of 4 see his four badges	**B.I.O. series 3** **Megumu Kasuga** > £1.50 each/£5 set of 4 see his four badges	**B.I.O. series 3** **Mimic** > £1.50 each/£5 set of 4 see his four badges	**B.I.O. series 3** **Nadine Faye James** > £1.50 each/£5 set of 4 see her four badges
B.I.O. series 3 **Rieme Gleijm** > £1.50 each/£5 set of 4 see her four badges	**B.I.O. series 3** **Vaughan Oliver @ v23** > £1.50 each/£4 set of 3 see his three badges	**B.I.O. series 3** **Vilderness** > £1.50 each/£4 set of 3 see his three badges	**B.I.O. series 3** **Yeong-Woong Cheong** > £1.50 each/£5 set of 4 see his four badges
B.I.O. (by invitation only) **button badge series 1** **SEE ALL 43 OF THEM**	**B.I.O.** (by invitation only) **button badge series 2** **SEE ALL 63 OF THEM**	**B.I.O.** (by invitation only) **button badge series 4** / NEW! **SEE ALL 41 OF THEM**	**Competition Winners** 2004 & 2005 **SEE ALL 20 OF THEM**

Stereohype™ graphic art & fashion boutique

clothes | graphic art | products | info | view basket

quantity: 0   total: £0.00

B.I.O. series 4 / NEW!
Anthony Burrill
> **£1.50** each/**£5** set of 4
see his four badges

B.I.O. series 4 / NEW!
Antoine + Manuel
> **£1.50** each/**£5** set of 4
see their four badges

B.I.O. series 4 / NEW!
FL@33
> **£1.50** each/**£5** set of 4
see their four badges

B.I.O. series 4 / NEW!
Geneviève Gauckler
> **£1.50**
see details

B.I.O. series 4 / NEW!
Hellohikimori
> **£1.50** each/**£4** set of 3
see their three badges

B.I.O. series 4 / NEW!
Jon Burgerman
> **£1.50** each/**£5** set of 4
see his four badges

B.I.O. series 4 / NEW!
Kerry Roper
> **£1.50** each/**£5** set of 4
see his four badges

B.I.O. series 4 / NEW!
Lunartik
> **£1.50** each/**£5** set of 4
see his four badges

B.I.O. series 4 / NEW!
Mark Adams
> **£1.50**
see details

B.I.O. series 4 / NEW!
Peskimo
> **£1.50** each/**£5** set of 4
see their four badges

B.I.O. series 4 / NEW!
Supermundane
> **£1.50** each/**£5** set of 4
see his four badges

B.I.O. series 4 / NEW!
Tabas
> **£1.50** each/**£5** set of 4
see his four badges

B.I.O. (by invitation only)
button badge series 1
SEE ALL 43 OF THEM

B.I.O. (by invitation only)
button badge series 2
SEE ALL 63 OF THEM

B.I.O. (by invitation only)
button badge series 3
SEE ALL 58 OF THEM

Competition Winners
2004 & 2005

Stereohype™ graphic art & fashion boutique

clothes | graphic art | products | info | view basket

quantity: 0   total: £0.00

Andy Steward
[single 2005]
earth > **£1.50**
see details

Dave Banks
[single 2005]
sap > **£1.50**
see details

Mauro Caramella
[single 2005]
clown > **£1.50**
see details

Emilie Baltz
[single 05]
f***ing flies > **£1.50**
see details

José Carlo Cunha
[series 2005]
> **£1.50** each/**£4** set of 3
see his three badges

Catalina Estrada
[series 2005]
> **£1.50** each/**£4** set of 3
see her three badges

Holly Wales
[series 2005]
> **£1.50** each/**£4** set of 3
see her three badges

Lars Kruse
[series 05]
> **£1.50** each/**£4** set of 3
see his three badges

Gary Barber
[2004] > **£1.50**
mr milk moustache
see details

Kate Forrester
[2004]
bird > **£1.50**
see details

J+E Design
[aka What What] [2004]
good gravy > **£1.50**
see details

Jonathan James Morris
[2004]
nipple > **£1.50**
see details

B.I.O. (by invitation only)
button badge series 1
SEE ALL 43 OF THEM

B.I.O. (by invitation only)
button badge series 2
SEE ALL 63 OF THEM

B.I.O. (by invitation only)
button badge series 3
SEE ALL 58 OF THEM

B.I.O. (by invitation only)
button badge series 4 / NEW!
SEE ALL 41 OF THEM

PROJECTBUTTON

Projectbutton began in 2001 when New Yorker Karyn Valino bought a badge-making machine and started to produce her own buttons. It's an online gallery featuring designs by dozens of international artists. Valino explains: "The idea was to create a collective, where artists from around the world could submit artwork which I would make into a button and then post in an online gallery. There is no fee or judging process, I make all submissions into buttons. People who participate can send in a dollar (to cover postage, parts, etc) and receive a randomly selected button from the collection made by another artist."

All buttons are displayed in the order submitted and each design is captioned to reveal the name of the artist, country of origin and a brief description of the design. Shown here are designs submitted by Lee Fenyves, Adam Jackson, Eileen Miffit, Dominic Relacion, Valino herself, and Kirk Weppler.

"The idea is to get a wide range of people from different backgrounds and countries to participate in an ongoing project," adds Valino. "The medium is the same, a one-inch button, yet the results are so widely different and creative."

www.projectbutton.com

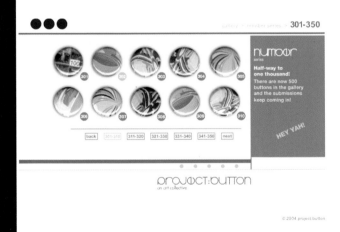

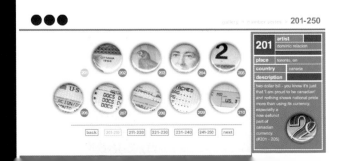

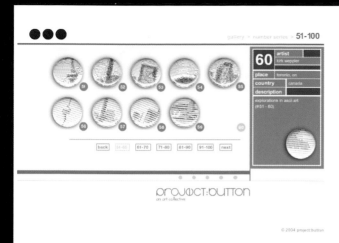

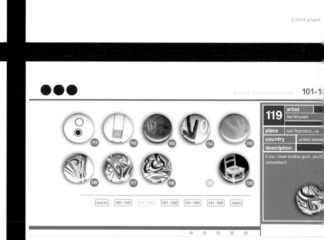

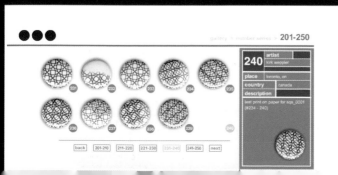

MAILING LIST

Insert email (subscribe / unsubscribe)   GO

THE COLLECTION
ABOUT PINPOPS
TERMS & CONDITIONS
CONTACT US

Electric Thought Activate!

ARTIST BADGES / APAK STUDIO

ALL CONTENT COPYRIGHT 2006 PINPOPS   E-COMMERCE ENGINE BUILT BY TAK! DESIGN

PINPOPS

Pinpops is a badge project set up by Dom
Murphy of Birmingham-based TAK! design
studio. Artists are asked to produce badges or
series of badges that will be unique to the
project. Shown here are screen grabs from the
site and also some of the first packs produced
and sold there. Artists who have designed for
Pinpops include Jon Burgerman, Peskimo,
Michael C. Place, Serge Seidlitz, Andy Smith
and Andrew Welland.

www.pinpops.com

MAILING LIST

Insert email (subscribe / unsubscribe)   GO

THE COLLECTION   VIEW ALL
ABOUT PINPOPS   ARTIST BADGES
TERMS & CONDITIONS
CONTACT US   SALE ITEMS

ALL MAJOR CREDIT AND DEBIT CARDS ACCEPTED VIA PAYPAL

ERGE SEIDLITZ

om-boys and Zom-girls for you to devour.

omly created via a special zombie
y TAK! as a follow up to their
. Each zombie is a mish mash of body
ale are 35 zombies from a possible
the destruction of any civilization!

nally showcased at the Monster Mash
Peskimo

TO ADD TO BASKET

MAILING LIST
Insert email (subscribe / unsubscribe)   GO

FILTER BY ARTIST
Display all

FILTER BY SEARCH
Search   GO

GO TO PAGE
PREV   2   NEXT

THE COLLECTION
ABOUT PINPOPS
TERMS & CONDITIONS
CONTACT US

ARTIST BADGES
SALE ITEMS

BLOG ROCK

£1.49

POLAROID

£1.49

TATTOO, TRUTH

Sold Out

APE MAN

Sold Out

TATTOO, MUM & DAD

Sold Out

TATTOO, SKULL

Sold Out

TATTOO, LOVE & HATE

Sold Out

I BELIEVE IN YOU

£1.49

ROBOT-O-CHAN

£1.49

POISON

Sold Out

GIRL

£1.49

I'M WITH BUILD

£1.49

SKULLY

£1.49

HELLO COMPUTER

£1.49

SAVE THE WOOLY MAMMOTH

£1.49

D*FACE

£1.49

SPORK

£1.49

ELECTRIC THOUGHT ACTIVATE!

£1.49

KILLER

£1.49

PYRO

Sold Out

MAILING LIST
Insert email (subscribe / unsubscribe)   GO

FILTER BY ARTIST
Display all

FILTER BY SEARCH
Search   GO

GO TO PAGE
1   NEXT

THE COLLECTION
ABOUT PINPOPS
TERMS & CONDITIONS
CONTACT US

ARTIST BADGES
SALE ITEMS

BIRD & TREE

£1.49

ZOMBIES

£1.49

WHAT GOES UP, MUST COME DOWN

Sold Out

FRANK

£1.49

GREGOR

£1.49

VINCE

£1.49

YOU ARE HERE

£2.49

ANATOMY LESSON

£1.49

I AM   ASTHMATIC

£1.49

HAND GESTURES: THE TREKKY

Sold Out

SMUT BUGS

£1.49

HAND GESTURES: ROCK SUICIDE

£1.49

IRON HELPS US LEARN!

£1.49

YES, I HAVE PORN

£1.49

CULPRIT

£1.49

CODY

£1.49 £0.99

BUGS

£1.49

PINPOP PROMO PACK

£2.49

JEAN BOGIEMAN

£1.49

FRIENDS & ENEMIES

£2.49

1   NEXT

MAILING LIST
Insert email (subscribe / unsubscribe)

THE COLLECTION
ABOUT PINPOPS
TERMS & CONDITIONS
CONTACT US

VIEW ALL
ARTIST BADGE
SALE ITEMS

ALL CONTENT COPYRIGHT 2006 PINPOPS

MAILING LIST
Insert email (subscribe / unsubscribe)

THE COLLECTION
ABOUT PINPOPS
TERMS & CONDITIONS
CONTACT US

VIEW ALL
ARTIST BA
SALE ITEM

Bird & Tree

ARTIST BADGES / ANDREW WELLAND

1inch metal pin badge

Delicious micro illustration from the talented Andy Welland. Expect more from this chap.

SELECT AN ITEM TO ADD TO BASKET	▼

ENGINE BUILT BY TAK! DESIGN

TAK! is a small but perfectly formed design and ideas factory based in Birmingham, UK.

TAK! believe in daydreaming and seek inspiration in up in the clouds.

Pinpops is an initiative and designed by TAK!

Visit website

VIEW ALL ITEMS BY TAK!

RUS ENG

pinpix service

INFO NEW | AVAILABLE | ALL

DESIGNERS:

All... ▼ sort

SPECIAL PROJECTS:

All... ▼ sort

Subscribe to the PINPIX newsletter:

@ [ ] Subscribe

Contact pinpix@gmail.com | XHTML/CSS
Copyright ©2005, All Rights Reserved

pinpix service
RUS ENG

PINPIX

Pinpix is a Russian website that launched in 2005 to feed Russian designers' and illustrators' love of the button badge. It already has well over 200 unique designs for visitors to browse and buy.

www.pinpix.ru
pinpix@gmail.com

ART

MARMALADE

Since its inception in November 2002, each issue of lifestyle magazine *Marmalade* has been themed. Issue number two had the theme Come Together and art director Sacha Spencer Trace used only three different materials in the page layouts: cloth, thread (embroidery) and badges.

All the badges in the Come Together spread belong to Spencer Trace and most, she tells us, were bought by her father at various car-boot sales in France. "I love badges and have hoarded them since I was seven years old," she reveals. "I think each is a beautifully graphic object, but I would only use them in context. Recently we've seen a lot of corporate/mainstream layout using badges as a 'way of communicating with yoof'. This is very similar to how graffiti was used/abused a few years ago. This really saddens me, as we could get to a point where badges become naff and lose their visual power/significance."

www.marmalademag.com

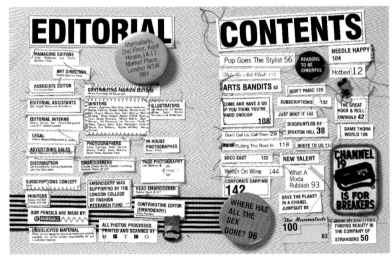

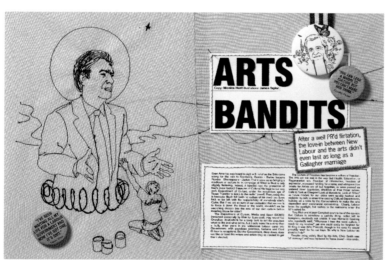

LOKI

London-based clothing company Loki sells a range of screenprinted T-shirts and sweatshirts in stores such as Magma and Bond International in London and also further afield in Brighton, Oxford and Stockholm. This particular design for its autumn/winter '06 range celebrates the small round format of the button badge and is based on classic slogan badges. The "badges" are screenprinted onto the material as artwork.

www.lokiclothing.co.uk

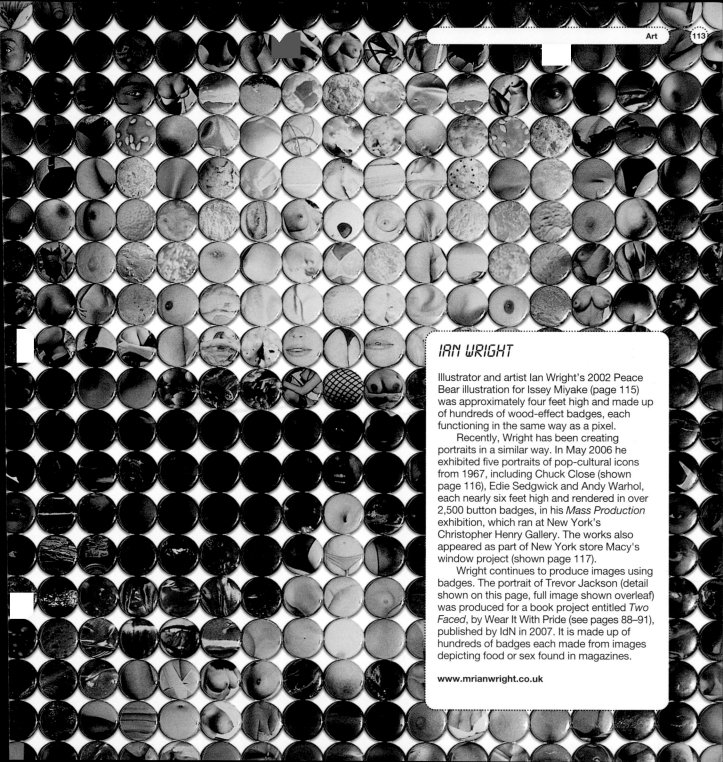

IAN WRIGHT

Illustrator and artist Ian Wright's 2002 Peace Bear illustration for Issey Miyake (page 115) was approximately four feet high and made up of hundreds of wood-effect badges, each functioning in the same way as a pixel.

Recently, Wright has been creating portraits in a similar way. In May 2006 he exhibited five portraits of pop-cultural icons from 1967, including Chuck Close (shown page 116), Edie Sedgwick and Andy Warhol, each nearly six feet high and rendered in over 2,500 button badges, in his *Mass Production* exhibition, which ran at New York's Christopher Henry Gallery. The works also appeared as part of New York store Macy's window project (shown page 117).

Wright continues to produce images using badges. The portrait of Trevor Jackson (detail shown on this page, full image shown overleaf) was produced for a book project entitled *Two Faced*, by Wear It With Pride (see pages 88–91), published by IdN in 2007. It is made up of hundreds of badges each made from images depicting food or sex found in magazines.

www.mrianwright.co.uk

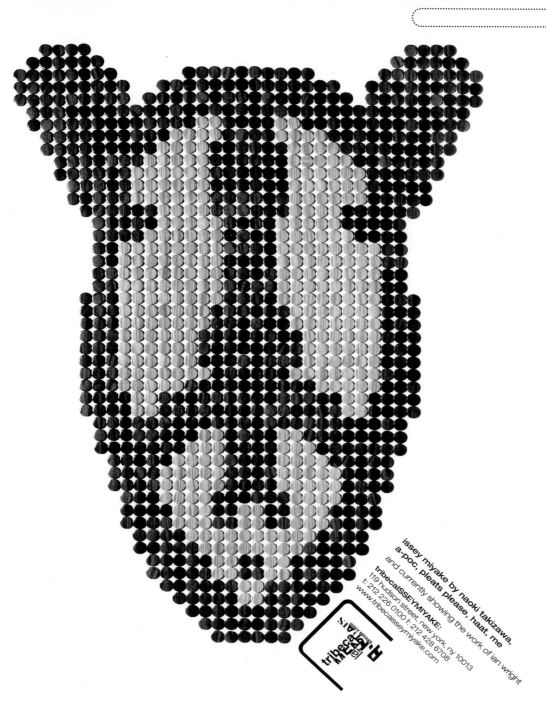

issey miyake by naoki takizawa,
a-poc, pleats please, haat, me
and currently showing the work of ian wright

tribecaISSEYMIYAKE:
119 hudson street, new york, ny 10013
t: 212 226 0100 f: 212 428 6708
www.tribecaisseymiyake.com

Supergrass is 10
The Best of 94–04

Featuring 21 classic tracks
including the hits:

Alright
Moving
Pumping On Your Stereo
Sun Hits The Sky
Grace
Going Out
Seen The Light
Late In The Day
Mansize Rooster
Richard III
Mary
and more...

7243 578994 1 3

SUPERGRASS IS 10

Created by YES studio art director Simon Earith while at Blue Source, the artwork for Supergrass' Supergrass Is 10 compilation album celebrates badge nostalgia. The initial idea, Earith explains, was to create a Supergrass Is 10 badge and photograph it as part of an imagined badge collection. However, Earith's research into the world of badges and badge collecting led him to the UK's most knowledgeable collector, Frank Setchfield at The Badge Collectors' Circle.

"Myself and my colleague Flack, who was producing the job, made a trip to Loughborough to visit Frank, drank milky tea, talked badges and looked through the thousands of badges in Frank's well-categorized collection," recalls Earith. "We were loaned a number of well-loved gems that were included on the sleeve, and we also remade a couple of impossible-to-find classics. The track listing was also illustrated with button badges – a badge was designed and then made up for each track on the record."

busworks www.bus-works.com
© Busworks Akiyoshi Chino / CWC

AKIYOSHI CHINO

Japanese illustrator Akiyoshi Chino specializes in character design. "I used to work as a production designer on character merchandising at a design firm, doing merchandising design and illustration for big-name characters like Hello Kitty," he explains. "After leaving my job at that company, I began work as a freelance designer and started developing my own characters, including Kumano Gollo. I am hoping to develop merchandise and multimedia projects using my original character designs."

Kumano Gollo, the lovable though absent-minded male bear character (who is, apparently, a master of Kumano-style judo), was actually entered into the Fresh Character Found competition held by artist agency CWC in 2004. Chino won the competition with his bouffant bear and confirms that, as a result, he is now signed to CWC and working with them on various projects to develop the Kumano Gollo character.

In June 2006 a mini-exhibition devoted to Kumano Gollo in the Fewmany store in Shinjuku saw T-shirts, button badges, mugs, illustrations, cushions and stickers featuring the character being displayed and sold.

www.bus-works.com
www.cwctokyo.com (Asia)
www.cwc-i.com (United States and Europe)

ONEINCHLOVE

Oneinchlove will soon be an up-and-running online destination for badges lovingly crafted by a host of designers. Just before a serious bike accident slowed down the site's development, its creator, Nick Cernis, sent out this promotional bag, adorned with badges by various designers including Blend (the design moniker of Cernis and his partner Hayley Thomas), Build, DEDass, iLovedust and TADO.

The Oneinchlove website is due to launch in spring 2007.

www.oneinchlove.com
www.designbybuild.com
www.tado.co.uk
www.dedass.com
www.studio-blend.com
www.ilovedust.com

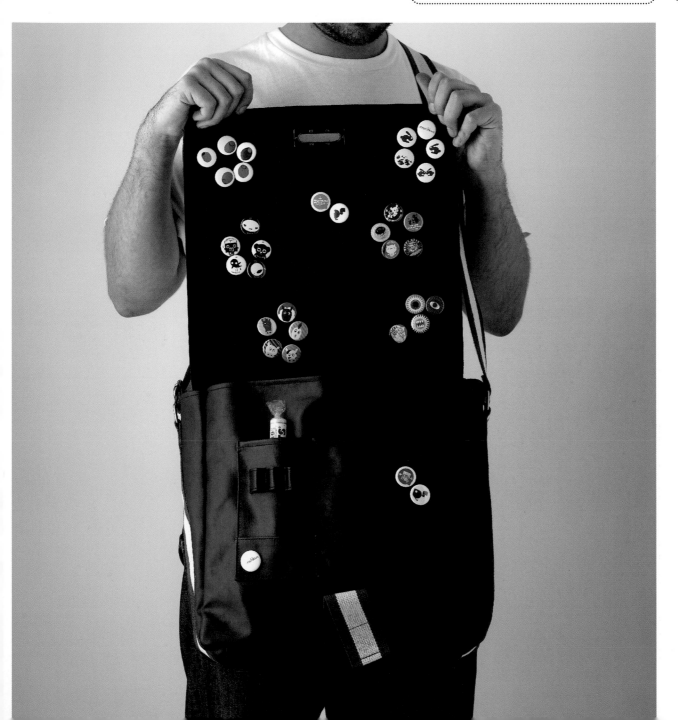

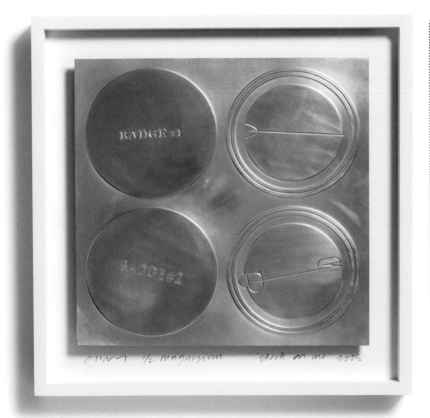

JONATHAN ELLERY

Jonathan Ellery, of London-based multi-discipline design consultancy Browns, created these embossed-metal artworks in response to being asked to produce work for a badge-focused exhibition entitled *Stuck On Me*, curated by Joana Niemeyer and Nadine Fleischer.

The exhibition ran at the Notting Hill Arts Club in the last two months of 2005 and included button badges and installations by a variety of badge enthusiasts including Daniel Eatock, Experimental Jetset, Peepshow, Spin and Zoo York.

"I produced two 'canvases', one made from solid three-gauge brass and the other in magnesium," explains Ellery. "They were crafted using precision-machining and CAD technology. More recently I've been experimenting with images in solid brass. I love the fact that it is very heavy and will be around long after I'm gone."

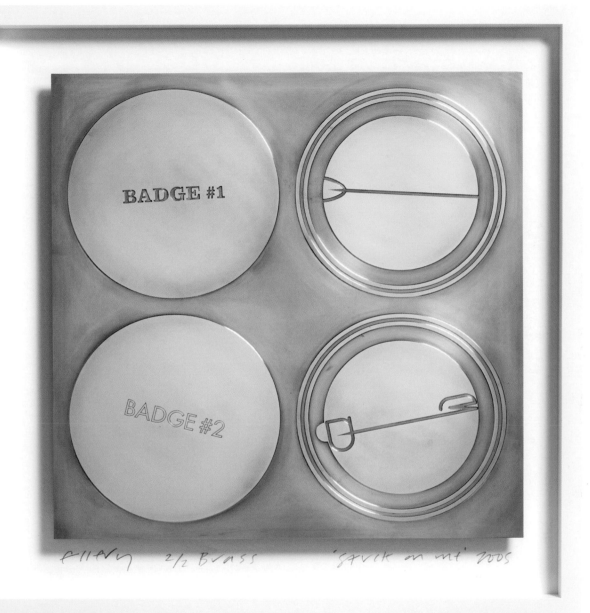

Acknowledgements

Thank you to all the people who responded so positively to the call for entries for this book and who sent badges from around the world. Thanks also to the designers and illustrators who not only designed badges specially for this book but who gave immeasurable encouragement and support: Agathe and Tomi at FL@33, Antoni & Alison, Fred Deakin, Gelman, Femke Hiemstra, Trevor Jackson, Kim Jones, Mark Pawson and Michael C. Place.

Without his input, encouragement and hard work, there would be no book – so particular thanks must go to *Badge/Button/Pin* designer Nathan Gale. And also to Jo Lightfoot and Robert Shore at Laurence King.

Sincere thanks also to: all at Airside, L'Amateur, Leona Baker, Roanne Bell, Polly Betton, Sir Peter Blake, Mark Blamire, Patrick Burgoyne, Maxim Cackett, Paula Carson, Eduardo Chavez, Linlee Allen and all at Colette, Anna and all at CWC, Mike Dorrian, Jonathan Ellery, Darren Firth, Nadine Fleischer, Francesca Gavin, Milton Glaser, David Henckel, It's Bigger Than, Karen Jane, James Joyce, Ravi Kajla, Chris Knight, Peter and Angela Lucas, Jennifer Lew, Daniel Lyons, Jeremy Mac Lynn, Colin McFarland, Dom Murphy, Austin and Matt at NEW, Joana Niemeyer, Marcus Oakley, Jodie and David at Peskimo, all at PSC Photography, Emmi Salonen, Frank Setchfield, Natasha Shah, Mark Sinclair, Sacha Spencer Trace, Louisa St Pierre, Lori Taylor, Jane Thomason, Karyn Valino, Helen Walters, The Waltons, Neal Whittington, Eliza Williams, Ian Wright and George Wu.

Special thanks to our families for all their support and encouragement and in particular to Ravi, Emma and Stanley.